The MAILBOX®
The Education Center®

Organize JANUARY Now!™

MW01259611

Everything You Need for a Successful January

Monthly Organizing Tools
Manage your time, classroom, and students with monthly organizational tools.

Essential Skills Practice
Practice essential skills this month with engaging activities and reproducibles.

January in the Classroom
Carry your monthly themes into every corner of the classroom.

Ready-to-Go Learning Centers and Skills Practice
Bring January to life right now!

Managing Editor: Sharon Murphy

Editorial Team: Becky S. Andrews, Kimberley Bruck, Karen P. Shelton, Diane Badden, Thad H. McLaurin, Kimberly Brugger-Murphy, Gerri Primak, Karen A. Brudnak, Hope Rodgers, Dorothy C. McKinney, Nancy Aquino, Rebecca Brudwick, Jill Davis, Stacie Stone Davis, Margaret Elliott, Cynthia Holcomb, Angie Kutzer, Beth Marquardt, Andrea Singleton, Leanne Stratton, Susan Walker, Katie Zuehlke

Production Team: Lisa K. Pitts, Pam Crane, Rebecca Saunders, David G. Bullard, Jennifer Tipton Cappoen, Chris Curry, Sarah Foreman, Theresa Lewis Goode, Clint Moore, Greg D. Rieves, Barry Slate, Donna K. Teal, Zane Williard, Tazmen Carlisle, Cat Collins, Marsha Heim, Amy Kirtley-Hill, Lynette Dickerson, Mark Rainey, Angela Kamstra, Sheila Krill

www.themailbox.com

Manufactured in the United States
10 9 8 7 6 5 4 3 2

Table of Contents

Monthly Organizing Tools
A collection of reproducible forms, notes, and other timesavers and organizational tools just for January.

Essential Skills Practice
Fun, skill-building activities and reproducibles that combine the skills your students must learn with favorite January themes.

January in the Classroom
In a hurry to find a specific type of January activity? It's right here!

Ready-to-Go Learning Centers and Skills Practice
Two center activities you can tear out and use almost instantly! Plus a collection of additional reproducible skill builders!

Skills Grid

	New Year	Martin Luther King Jr. Day	Winter	Polar Animals	Centers	Games	Time Fillers	Writing Ideas & Prompts	Learning Center: Let It Snow!	Learning Center: The Polar Plunge	Ready-to-Go Skills Practice
Literacy											
letter identification						62					
matching uppercase and lowercase letters			30								91
initial consonants: *p, s*				48							
initial consonant: *m*											90
short vowels: *a, o*											92
short and long vowels					59						
word families			32								
sight words			33								
rhyming	19			43							
segmenting words				40							
syllables					58						
adding *-ing*			39								
spelling							69				
vocabulary						63					
opposites			37								
writing	18	25		41				70, 71			
rebus writing								71			
telling and asking sentences											93
sequencing a story in four steps										82, 89	
speaking		26					69				
skill review			31								
Math											
number identification				41							
counting							68				
counting backward	19										
counting by fives				49							
number order to 100											95
ordinal numbers				43							
numerals and sets			30								
match numbers to sets					58						
comparing sets				40							
comparing numbers			32								
estimation			33								
building numbers					59						
sums to 20			31								
subtraction	20	29									
subtraction to 10										74	
subtraction to 18										74, 81	
addition and subtraction facts						62					
addition and subtraction facts to 12											96
nonstandard measurement				42							
time to the hour	22										
using a calendar	23										
identifying pennies and nickels											94
spatial skills		24									
graphing			38								
patterns	18										
skill review			31								
Social Studies											
character education	20										
origins of a holiday		24									
appreciate differences between people		25									
appreciate the similarities among people		26									
Science											
characteristics of living things				42							
air resistance							68				
Physical Development											
gross motor						63					

Medallion
Tape to a student's clothing or to a crepe paper necklace.

Brag Tag
Use a child's words to finish the sentence starter.

I'm all smiles because…

©The Mailbox® • *Organize January Now!*™ • TEC60979

Award

_____
name

had a perfect performance in

_____
subject

_____
teacher

_____
date

©The Mailbox® • *Organize January Now!*™ • TEC60979

Medallion, brag tag, and award: Copy onto colorful construction paper, cut out, and use as desired.

January

Sunday	Monday	Tuesday	Wednesday	Thursday	Friday	Saturday

Center Checklist

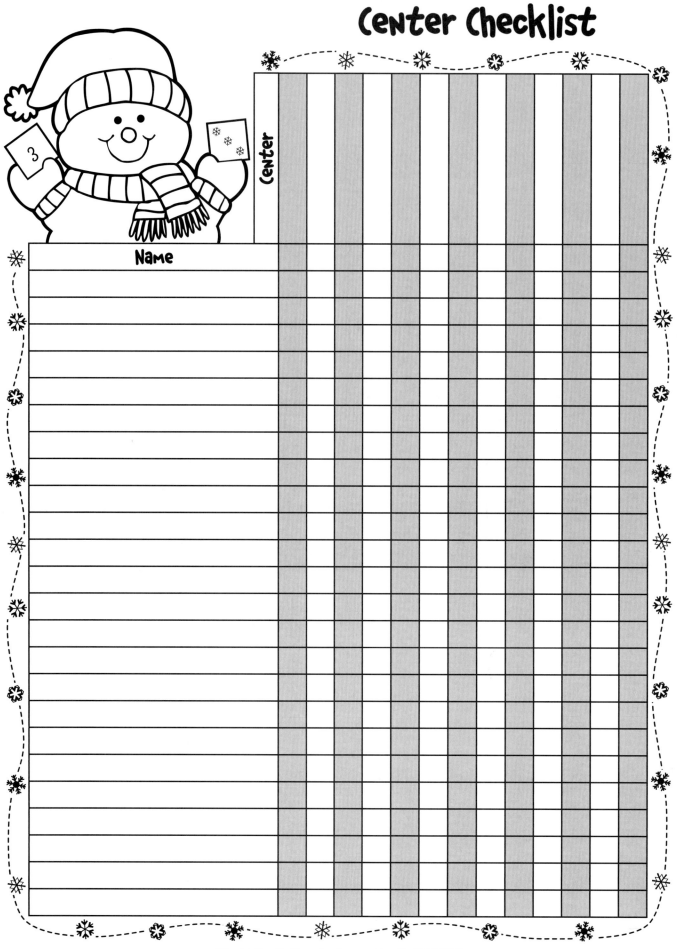

Center

Name

CLASS LIST

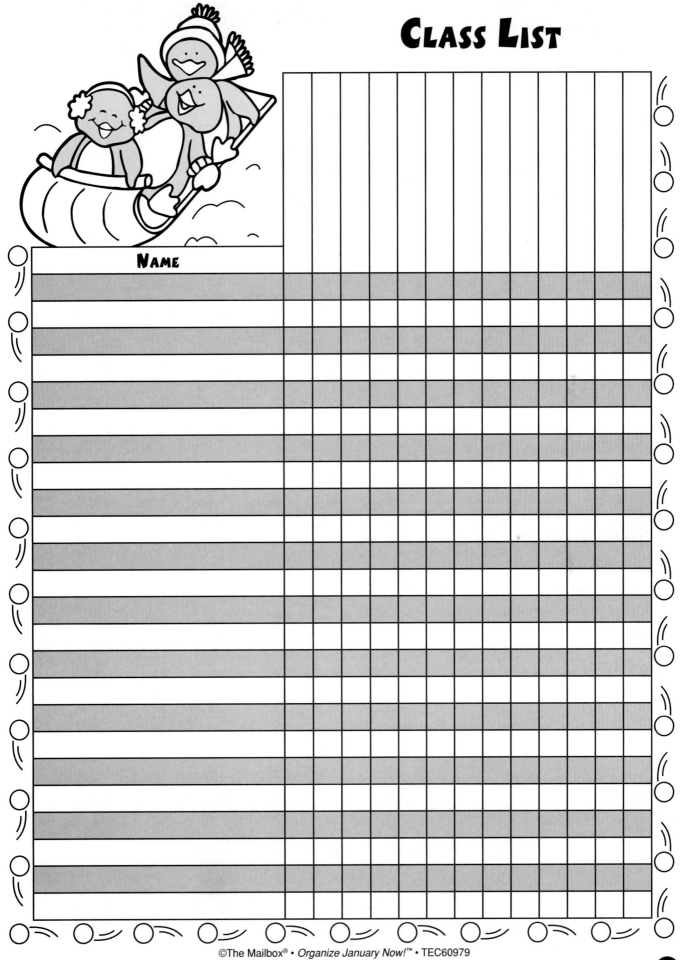

NAME											

Classroom News

From _____

Date _____

Please Remember

Look What We Are Learning

Superstars

Special Thanks

Help Wanted

Classroom News

Date _____

From _____

News

HAPPY NEW YEAR!

Clip art: Use the artwork on student papers and on correspondence such as announcements, forms, and parent notes.

Name _____

Goal _____

Hooray for you!

©The Mailbox® • *Organize January Now!*™ • TEC60979

Cool!

Name _____

Goal _____

©The Mailbox® • *Organize January Now!*™ • TEC60979

Name _____

Goal _____

_____

You can do it!

©The Mailbox® • *Organize January Now!*™ • TEC60979

Incentive charts: Have students track their progress as they work toward a variety of goals.

My Journal

Name _____

Journal cover: Make this page the front cover of your students' writing journals.

Materials to Collect:

Duties This Month:

Meetings:

Birthdays & Special Dates:

To Do:

✴_____
✴_____
✴_____
✴_____
✴_____
✴_____
✴_____
✴_____
✴_____
✴_____
✴_____
✴_____

Themes:

©The Mailbox® • *Organize January Now!*™ • TEC60979

Monthly planning form: Use this handy form to stay on top of January's school-related responsibilities.

 **Monthly Organizing Tools**

Open page: Use this page for parent correspondence or with students. For example, ask each child to write (or dictate as you write) about things that come in pairs (like mittens) or whether he would rather wear mittens or gloves.

Dear Parent,

Please remember

_____
date

Thanks!

SCHOOL NOTE

School Note

School notes: Use these notes for parent communications, such as announcing an upcoming event, requesting supplies or volunteers, and writing messages of praise.

Energize a winter day with this colorful booklet. Help your child read the text on the cover and on each booklet page. Have him or her write a different color word on each line and draw the object in the featured color. Next, have your child color the booklet cover and then cut it out along with the booklet pages. Sequence the cover and pages and then staple or tape them together. Finally, invite your child to read the book again before returning it to school.

We hope to see the completed project by _____.

Sincerely,

Winter Wear

by _____

©The Mailbox® • *Organize January Now!*™ • TEC60979

_____ hat ①

_____ boots ②

_____ coat ③

Learning Links: color words, reading

Note to the teacher: Date and sign a copy of the page. Then make student copies on white construction paper. Have each child write his name on the booklet cover before taking the page home. When a child returns the project, encourage him to read his booklet to his classmates.

Monthly Organizing Tools **17**

New Year

Math

Colorful Confetti

To make a supply of confetti, have students cut one-inch strips of colorful construction paper into smaller pieces of different shapes and sizes. Next, direct each child to use the confetti to make a grade-appropriate color pattern. Then have her glue the pattern to a length of crepe paper. After the glue dries, display these festive streamers throughout the classroom to welcome the new year!

Writing Literacy

Looking Forward, Looking Back

With this two-sided mirror, youngsters can look back at accomplishments of the past year and look forward to future achievements in the new year. To prepare, give each child a large tagboard oval (trimmed from a 9" x 12" sheet of tagboard), two sheets of aluminum foil large enough to cover the oval, two copies of the mirror pattern on page 21, and a copy of the word strips on page 21.

To make a mirror, a child glues a sheet of foil to each side of the oval and trims off the excess foil. Then he glues a word strip to each mirror pattern and completes each mirror with a corresponding sentence and illustration. Next, he glues a mirror to each side of the foil-covered oval and tapes on a large craft stick handle. Encourage youngsters to share their mirrors with each other before taking them home.

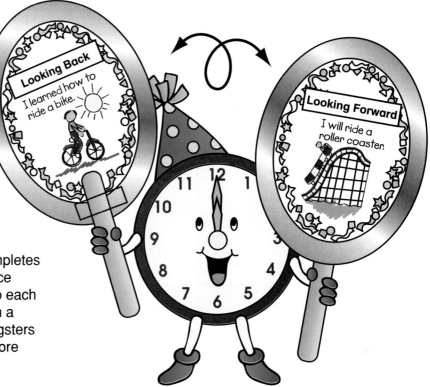

Looking Back
I learned how to ride a bike.

Looking Forward
I will ride a roller coaster.

Start the new year off with a bang when you incorporate these skill-based ideas into your curriculum!

Rhyming • Literacy

Happy Moo Year?

When youngsters replace the word *new* in *new year,* their imaginations will soar! To begin, enlist students' help in compiling a list of words that rhyme with *new.* Lead youngsters to notice that not all of the words have the same ending. Then direct each child to choose a rhyming word from the list. Give him a sheet of paper and have him copy the title "Happy _____ Year," inserting the chosen word in the blank. Encourage him to draw a picture that corresponds with his title. Display these giggle-inducing New Year's greetings for all to see!

Suggestions		
chew	flew	grew
stew	glue	two
clue	blue	shoe
boo	moo	zoo

Math • • • • • • • • • • • • • • • • • • Counting backward

Countdown

Explain to youngsters that counting down from ten is a common custom done on New Year's Eve as the ball drops in Times Square in New York City. To prepare for your own class countdown, program ten large cards each with a different number from 1 to 10. Give each of ten students a different card and give one student a ball. Have youngsters work together to line themselves up in backward order from 10 to 1, with the student holding the ball beside 1. Encourage the seated students to verify their classmates' order and then count down from ten as each standing student holds up her card. After students say, "One," the child holding the ball drops it while the class cheers. Repeat the activity, making sure to give each child an opportunity to hold a number card.

10, 9, 8, 7, 6, 5, 4, 3, 2, 1!

· **Subtraction**

Pleasing Party Hats

Prepare a class supply of large construction paper triangles to resemble party hats. Gather four different hat decorations such as pom-poms, tissue paper squares, large sequins, and stickers. Also prepare a recording sheet similar to the one shown. Place a class supply of recording sheets, party hats, decorations, two dice, and glue at a center.

When a child visits the center, she rolls the dice and writes the corresponding subtraction fact in the first box of a recording sheet. She determines the difference, takes the matching number of decorations, and glues them to her hat. (If the difference rolled is zero, she takes another turn.) Play continues until the recording sheet is complete. After the glue dries, staple the hat to a paper strip and size the strip to make a headband.

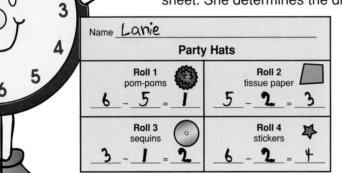

Name: Lanie

Party Hats

Roll 1 pom-poms	Roll 2 tissue paper
6 − 5 = 1	5 − 2 = 3
Roll 3 sequins	**Roll 4** stickers
3 − 1 = 2	6 − 2 = 4

Social Studies

Character education · · · · · · · · · · · · · · · · · ·

Our Pledge

Youngsters pledge to keep a class resolution with this banner project. After discussing the tradition of making a New Year's resolution, enlist students' help in creating a group resolution. To make a banner, write the chosen resolution on a large sheet of bulletin board paper. Then invite one student at a time to the banner, paint his hand, and have him make a handprint on the banner. (Write each student's name lightly with pencil next to his handprint.) After all of the handprints are dry, have a few students at a time use permanent markers to personalize, decorate, and write the new year on their handprints. Display the banner to remind youngsters of their pledge.

We will clean up after lunch every day.

Find reproducible activities on pages 22–23.

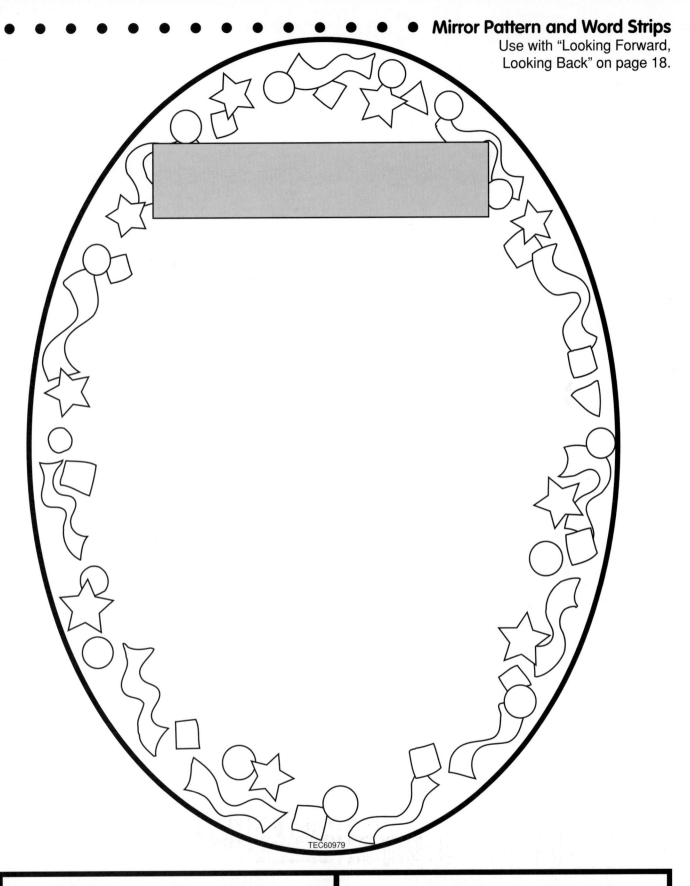

TEC60979

Looking Forward	Looking Back

Time to Celebrate!

Name _____

🖍 Color each box that shows the correct time.

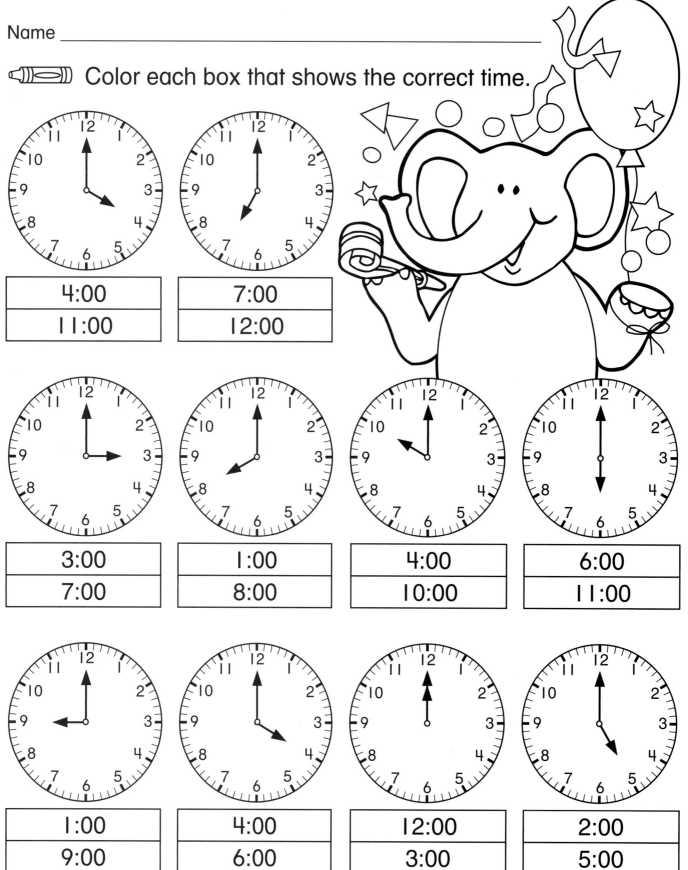

4:00	7:00
11:00	12:00

3:00	1:00	4:00	6:00
7:00	8:00	10:00	11:00

1:00	4:00	12:00	2:00
9:00	6:00	3:00	5:00

Dailey's Dates

Name _____

Fill in the calendar for this month.

_____
month

Sunday	Monday	Tuesday	Wednesday	Thursday	Friday	Saturday
					Birthday	
			Dentist			
Bath						

Read and do.

① Write how many days are in this month. _____

② Write the date that Dailey goes to the dentist. _____

_____

③ Write the date of Dailey's birthday. _____

_____

④ Dailey gets a bone on the **third** Monday. Draw a 🦴 on that date.

⑤ Color the date **after** Dailey's birthday red.

⑥ Color the date **before** Dailey's bath blue.

Note to the teacher: If extra calendar boxes are needed, divide the appropriate number of boxes on the bottom row before making student copies.

Using a Calendar ㉓

Martin Luther King Jr. Day

Social Studies

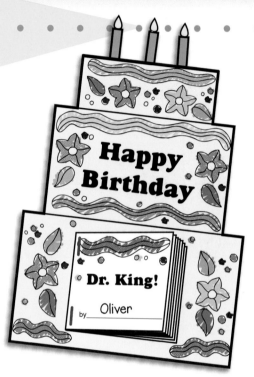

Origins of a holiday

Happy Birthday Booklet

In celebration of Dr. King's birthday, have students make these festive booklets. Instruct each child to color and cut out a construction paper copy of the cake pattern on page 27. Next, direct each student to color and cut out a copy of the booklet cover and pages on page 28. Help him stack the cover and pages in order and staple them to the cake where indicated. If desired, have students add construction paper candles to the top of the cake. Then invite student volunteers to read through the booklet as their classmates follow along in their own copies.

Spatial skills

Math

A Hidden Message

When students put together this heart-shaped puzzle, they'll find information about Martin Luther King Jr.! Make a large heart cutout from red bulletin board paper. Write the information shown on the cutout. Then puzzle-cut the heart into several pieces and place it at a center along with a supply of writing paper and pencils. Encourage each child to visit the center and put the puzzle together. Then have her read the information and write it on a sheet of paper. When you see the student's paper, you'll know that she's put together the heart puzzle and learned something about Dr. King!

Dr. King was a kind man. He wanted people to love each other.

Commemorate the birthday of Martin Luther King Jr. with this selection of ideas that celebrate his message of peace and friendship.

Appreciate differences between people

Celebrating Differences

In honor of Martin Luther King, create this display to show the uniqueness of individuals. Cut out a supply of circles in a variety of skin tones. To begin, have each youngster share information about her achievements or interests as you write the information in the center of a piece of bulletin board paper. Next, encourage each child to choose a prepared circle and use crayons and yarn pieces to transform it into a self-portrait. When the glue is dry, attach the faces to the bulletin board paper to resemble a frame. Display the paper with the title "Celebrate Our Differences!"

Max can jump really high.
Derek plays soccer.
Shana is taking dance lessons.
Carla likes to paint.
Trevor likes to ride his bike.
Haley collects stamps.
Taylor loves cats.
Genna likes to collect rocks.
Duane likes to draw.
Ashley plays T-ball.

Handsome Doves

Have each child press his hands in a shallow pan of white tempera paint. Then direct him to make white handprints on a sheet of 9" x 12" construction paper, helping him place his hands so that the thumbs slightly overlap as shown. Fill in any blank areas with white paint. Then encourage him to glue hole-punched eyes and an orange beak cutout to the prints to make a dove. When the paint is dry, explain that people think of peace when they see a dove. Tell students that the word *peace* means "freedom from fighting, arguing, or bad feelings." Encourage each child to write one way he plans to be a peaceful person underneath his dove. Then display these projects on a wall or bulletin board.

I will be peaceful. I will not fight with others.

Social Studies

How are people the same?

They have ears.
They have noses.
They laugh.
They cry.
They want to have friends.
They have knees.
They like to have fun.

Appreciate the similarities among people

Same on the Inside

In the spirit of Dr. King's beliefs, use this activity to show the sameness that we all share. Have youngsters describe ways that people are the same; write their ideas on a sheet of chart paper. Next, present a red potato and a white potato. Have students describe how the potatoes are different. Then show them a peeled red potato and a peeled white potato. Ask the students whether they can determine which potato is red and which is white, leading them to conclude that the insides of the potatoes look alike. Then explain that the two potatoes are a lot like people—they may look different on the outside, but on the inside they're very much the same!

Speaking

Literacy

Ode to Dr. King

Invite students to share what they know about Dr. King. After each volunteer finishes sharing, sing a joyous round of the song shown.

*(sung to the tune of
"When the Saints Go Marching In")*

Oh, when we sing of Dr. King,
Oh, when we sing of Dr. King,
We will remember his kind message
When we sing of Dr. King.

Find a reproducible activity
on page 29.

Happy Birthday

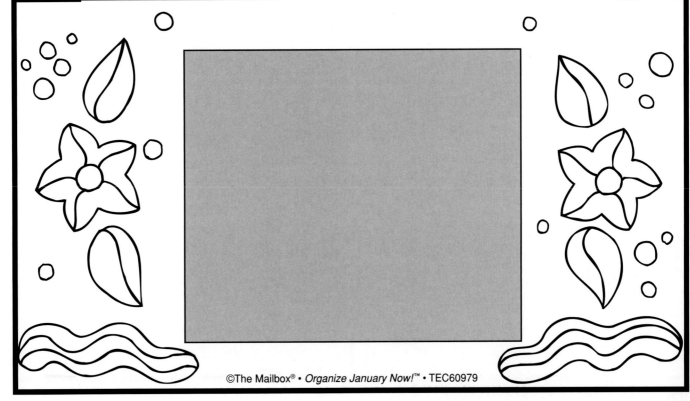

Dr. King!

by _____

©The Mailbox® • *Organize January Now!*™ • TEC60979

Dr. King was a preacher at a church. 1

He believed that all people should live in peace. 2

Dr. King led a bus boycott. 3

He gave speeches and changed laws. 4

We remember Dr. King every year in January. 5

Dr. King's Dream

Name _____

Subtract.

Match the letters to the numbered lines below to solve the riddle.

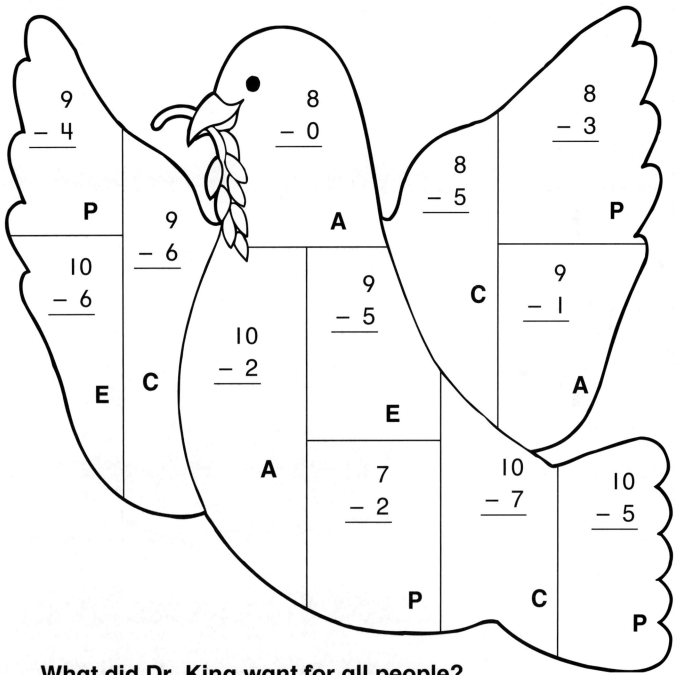

$$
\begin{array}{r} 9 \\ -\ 4 \\ \hline \end{array}
$$
P

$$
\begin{array}{r} 10 \\ -\ 6 \\ \hline \end{array}
$$
E

$$
\begin{array}{r} 9 \\ -\ 6 \\ \hline \end{array}
$$
C

$$
\begin{array}{r} 8 \\ -\ 0 \\ \hline \end{array}
$$
A

$$
\begin{array}{r} 10 \\ -\ 2 \\ \hline \end{array}
$$
A

$$
\begin{array}{r} 9 \\ -\ 5 \\ \hline \end{array}
$$
E

$$
\begin{array}{r} 7 \\ -\ 2 \\ \hline \end{array}
$$
P

$$
\begin{array}{r} 8 \\ -\ 5 \\ \hline \end{array}
$$
C

$$
\begin{array}{r} 8 \\ -\ 3 \\ \hline \end{array}
$$
P

$$
\begin{array}{r} 9 \\ -\ 1 \\ \hline \end{array}
$$
A

$$
\begin{array}{r} 10 \\ -\ 7 \\ \hline \end{array}
$$
C

$$
\begin{array}{r} 10 \\ -\ 5 \\ \hline \end{array}
$$
P

What did Dr. King want for all people?

___ ___ ___ ___ ___
 5   4   8   3   4

Winter

Math • • • • • • • • • • • • • • Numerals and sets

Frosty Fellows

The result of this partner game is two snazzy snowpals! Have each child cut out a copy of the snowpal patterns on page 34. To take a turn, a player rolls a large die and counts the dots. After he announces the number, he finds the matching snowpal pattern and places it on a sheet of blue paper. (If there isn't a corresponding pattern left, his turn is over.) Play continues until each player builds a snowpal. Invite youngsters to glue their patterns to their papers and decorate their snowpals as desired.

Matching uppercase and lowercase letters • • • • • • • • • Literacy

Hit the Slopes!

For this center, program pairs of craft sticks with corresponding uppercase and lowercase letters. Place the resulting skis at a center that you've decorated with a white sheet to resemble a ski slope. If desired, add cotton batting for snow. A child matches the uppercase and lowercase letters and places each pair of skis on the slope.

The weather outside may be frightful, but these skill-based ideas celebrating winter are delightful!

Skill review • • • • • • • • • • • • • • • • •

Finger Figure Skating

Reinforce a variety of skills with this wintry activity. Give each child a sheet of aluminum foil with a dollop of shaving cream to represent snow on a frozen lake. Invite youngsters to spread the snow over the lake with their hands. Then announce a skill, such as one of the ones shown, and have students "finger skate" to write the answer. Add more snow to the lakes as needed.

Suggestions

Write a word's beginning, middle, or ending sound.

Write sums or differences.

Write sight words.

Form letters or numerals.

Math • • • • • • • • • • • • • • • • • • *Sums to 20*

Name: Madison

Snowy Sums

A. $4 + 8 = 12$ B. ___ + ___ = ___
C. ___ + ___ = ___   D. ___ + ___ = ___
E. ___ + ___ = ___   F. ___ + ___ = ___
G. ___ + ___ = ___   H. ___ + ___ = ___

Shoveling Sums

To prepare this center, place 20 large white pom-poms or cotton balls (snowballs) in a shoebox or similar container. Place the box, copies of the recording sheet on page 36, a small plastic shovel, and pencils at a center. A child shovels one scoop of snowballs, counts them, and writes the corresponding number on the recording sheet. Then she shovels another scoop of snowballs and completes the addition fact. To check her answer, she counts all of the snowballs. After she places the snowballs back in the box, she continues making addition facts for the remaining spaces on her recording sheet.

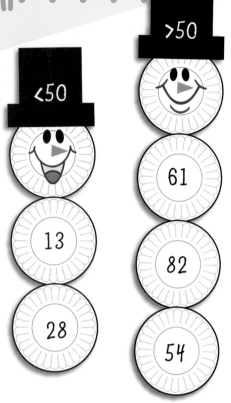

Chilly Numbers

Students build number skills and two jolly snowmen with this frosty activity. Select a grade-appropriate number you would like students to compare with other numbers. Label each of two black construction paper top hats with the number and an inequality symbol. Glue each hat to a different small paper plate and draw a face on each plate. Attach the plates side by side on the wall. Program several other paper plates with numbers that are greater than or less than the chosen number. Gather students near the display and have students, in turn, attach the plates below the appropriate symbol to build two snowpals. Repeat the activity by simply changing the number on the hats.

Word families

Literacy

A Wintry Word Wheel

Make a copy of the wheel patterns on page 35. Program the larger wheel with a chosen rime and the smaller wheel with different onsets for the word family. (If there are not enough onsets to fill up the spaces, repeat them as needed.) Copy the programmed wheels onto tagboard to make a class supply. Have each child cut out a copy of the programmed wheels. Then help her attach the smaller wheel atop the larger wheel with a brad.

To begin, say a word from the chosen word family and have each child manipulate the wheel to make that word. Then instruct her to run her finger under the word while orally blending the onset and rime together. Continue in this manner for the remaining words. If desired, pair students and have each partner take a turn saying a word while the other forms it on her wheel.

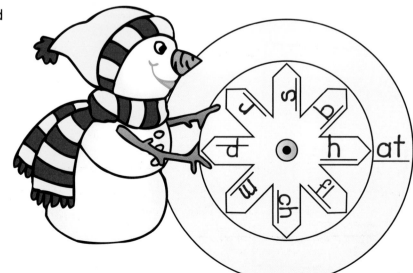

• • • • • • • • • • • •

In the Snow

To create this frosty center, use a bottle of white glue to write a different sight word on each of several white cards. After the glue dries, the resulting word will almost blend in with the card, as if it is hidden in the snow. Then cut white paper to be the same size as the cards. Place at a center the word cards, the pieces of paper, and crayons with the paper removed. A child places a piece of paper atop a word card and rubs a crayon over it to reveal the hidden sight word. She reads the word and continues in this manner for the remaining words. Encourage her to take home her word rubbings for extra sight word practice.

• • • • • • • • • • • • • •

How Big?

For this whole-group activity, trim a sheet of white bulletin board paper into an igloo shape. Cut out enough identical light blue paper ice blocks to cover the entire igloo. Present the igloo and one ice block to students. Have each child estimate how many ice blocks will fit on the igloo without overlapping; then have him write his estimate on a sticky note. After each youngster shares his estimate, enlist students' help in covering the igloo with ice blocks and counting them. Then have each student categorize his estimate by attaching his sticky note to a chart similar to the one shown. Challenge more advanced students to find the difference between their estimates and the actual count.

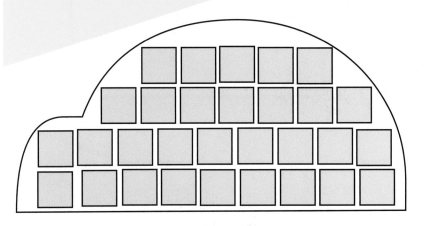

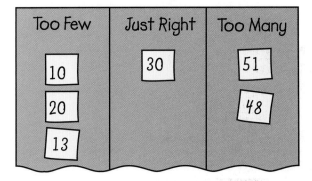

Too Few	Just Right	Too Many
10	30	51
20		48
13		

Find reproducible activities on pages 37–39.

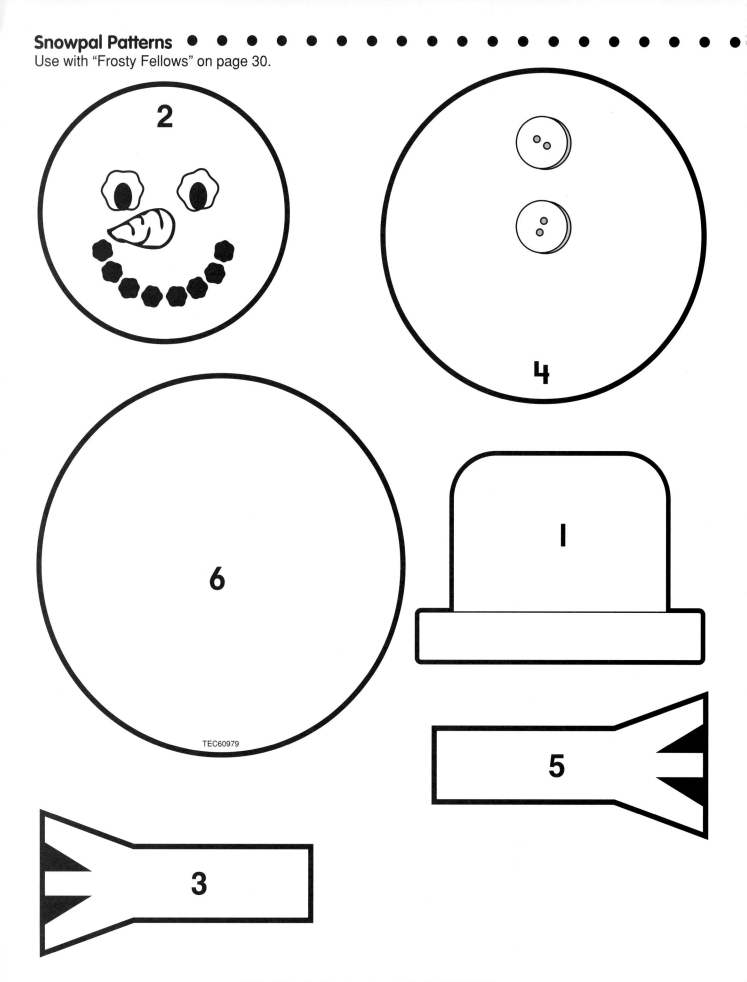

TEC60979

TEC60979

Name _____

Snowy Sums

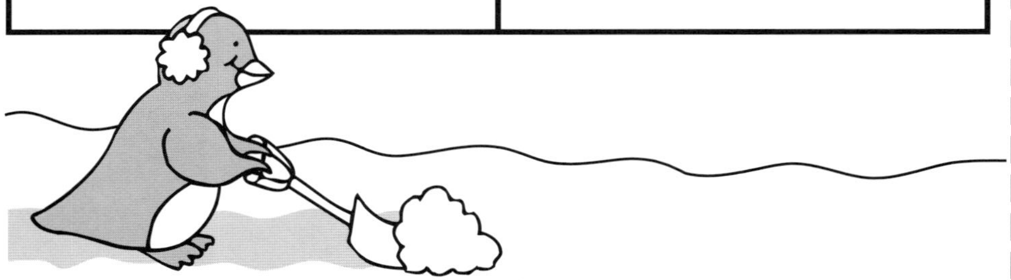

A. ___ + ___ = ___	B. ___ + ___ = ___
C. ___ + ___ = ___	D. ___ + ___ = ___
E. ___ + ___ = ___	F. ___ + ___ = ___
G. ___ + ___ = ___	H. ___ + ___ = ___

Note to the teacher: Use with "Shoveling Sums" on page 31.

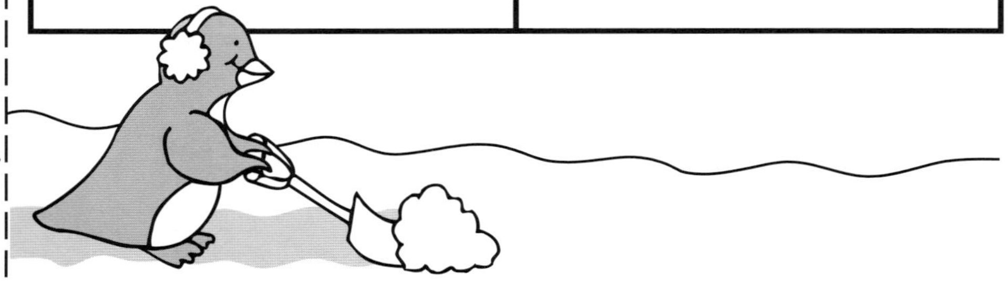

Name _____

Snowy Sums

A. ___ + ___ = ___	B. ___ + ___ = ___
C. ___ + ___ = ___	D. ___ + ___ = ___
E. ___ + ___ = ___	F. ___ + ___ = ___
G. ___ + ___ = ___	H. ___ + ___ = ___

A Happy Hare

Name _____

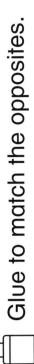

✂ Cut.

Glue to match the opposites.

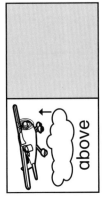 above

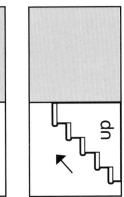 up

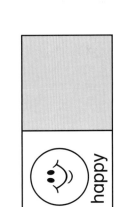 happy

hot

day

empty

tall

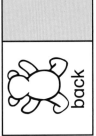 big

 back

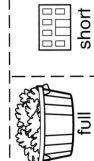 down

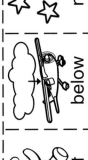 short

 full

 sad

 small

cold

night

below

front

Opposites 37

Mitten Mix-Up

Name _____

Count the mittens.

Color the graph.

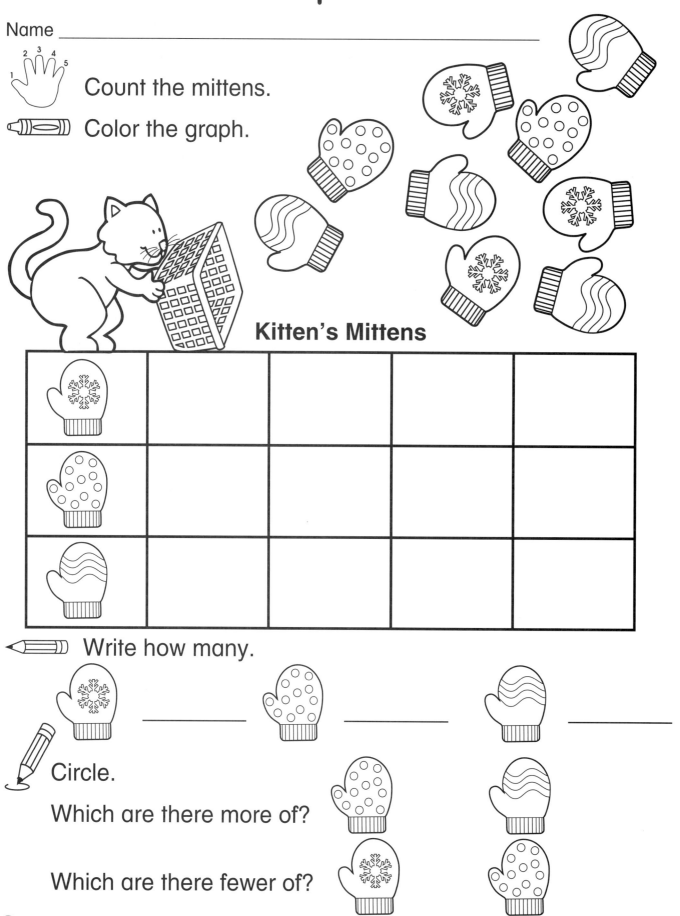

Kitten's Mittens

Write how many.

_____   _____   _____

Circle.

Which are there more of?

Which are there fewer of?

Falling Snow

Name _____

Use **ing** to make new words.

Write.

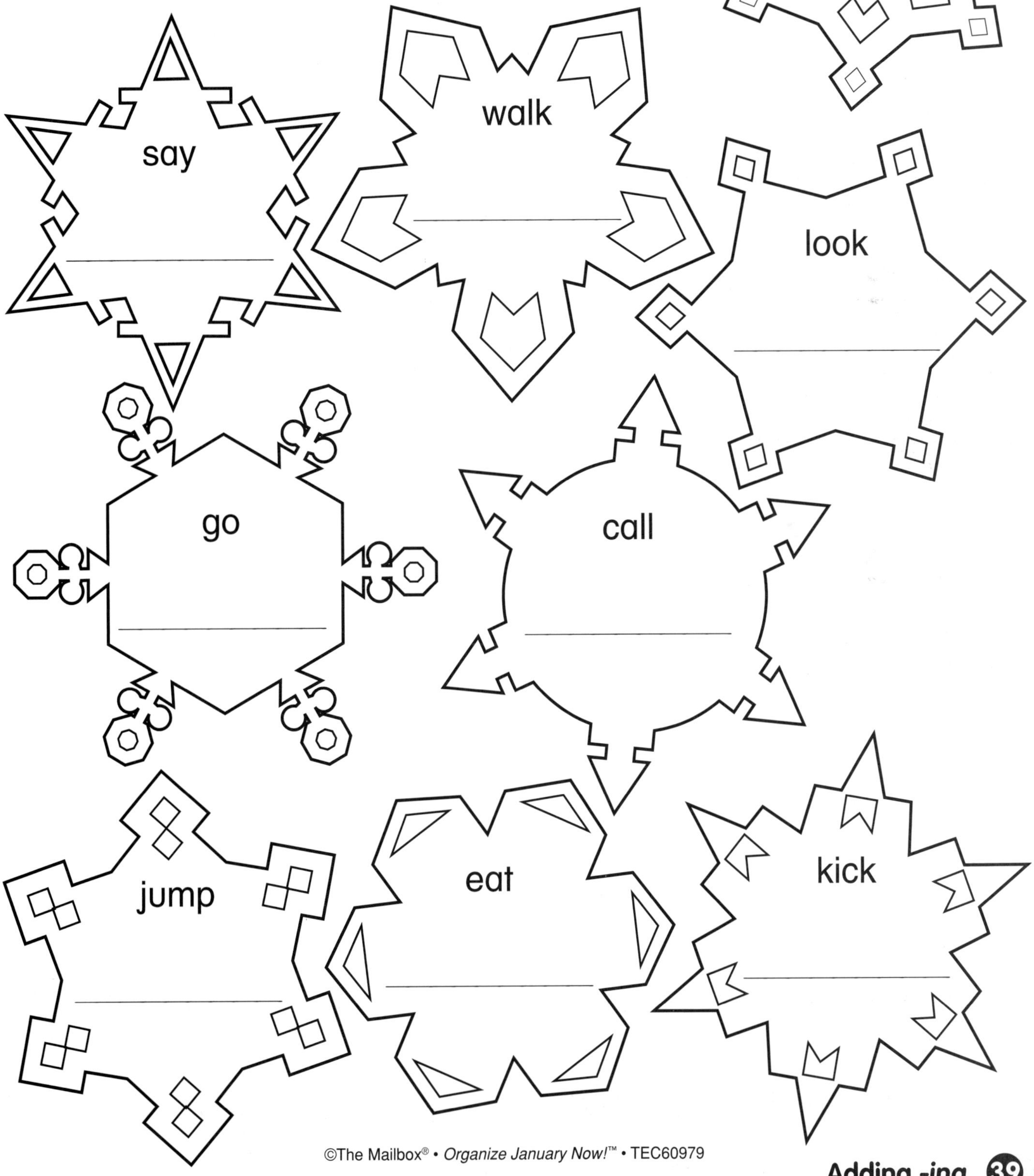

say
_____

walk
_____

look
_____

go
_____

call
_____

jump
_____

eat
_____

kick
_____

Polar Animals

Literacy

f-i-sh

Sound Count

With this sweet activity, youngsters segment animal names into their individual sounds! Give each child a small cup of miniature marshmallows (icebergs) and a strip of blue construction paper (water). Slowly say the name of a polar animal, such as a fox, seal, hare, fish, bear, or whale. Encourage each youngster to segment the animal's name by "floating" an iceberg on her water for each sound she hears. Count the sounds as a group to check for accuracy. Then continue in the same way with other animal names. When youngsters are finished with the activity, invite them to snack on their icebergs.

Comparing sets

Math

Let's Eat!

Students may be surprised to find out that puffins, small Arctic-dwelling birds, swim underwater to catch their favorite food—fish! Have youngsters compare the catches of two different puffins with this neat activity! Cut out two sets of the fish cards and two copies of the puffin pattern on page 44. Display the puffins on a flat surface in front of a small group of children. Invite a child to roll a die and then place the corresponding number of fish on a puffin. Encourage a second child to repeat the process, placing the appropriate number of fish on the second puffin. Have the remaining youngsters determine which puffin caught more fish and which caught fewer fish. Continue in this same manner for a desired number of rounds.

Bring polar animals onto the scene with this cool collection of cross-curricular activities!

Polar Pals

A cool mascot provides plenty of writing inspiration! Stock a small cooler with a stuffed polar animal, a personalized copy of the journal page on page 45, and a note of explanation to parents. Send the cooler home with the child. When the youngster returns the cooler, invite him to read his writing and add the page to a class journal. Then place a new personalized journal page in the cooler and have a different youngster take it home.

Dear Family,
    A polar pal has come to visit! Have your child include the animal in his or her activities throughout the evening. Then encourage your youngster to write about the experience on the journal paper provided. Place the animal and the journal page in the cooler and send it back to school. We can't wait to see what adventures our polar pal has with your child!

Searching for Seals

This game of hide-and-seek has youngsters identifying numbers while they look for little seals! Use the patterns on page 46 to make four gray construction paper seals. Cut out 20 iceberg shapes from white construction paper and program each one with a different number. Arrange the icebergs in a pocket chart. Then, as youngsters cover their eyes, hide each seal behind a different iceberg. Ask students to open their eyes, and encourage a child to point to an iceberg and read the number. Then instruct her to remove the iceberg to see if a seal is hiding behind it. If so, have her classmates give her a "seal" of approval by flapping their hands. Continue until all of the seals have been found. Then have students cover their eyes as you hide the seals behind different numbers and repeat the activity.

Penguin Particulars

To make this booklet, give each child a copy of the booklet backing on page 46 and a copy of page 47. Have each student color and cut out the booklet backing. Instruct her to use the word bank to complete each booklet page before cutting out the cover and pages. Help her stack the pages in order with the cover on top. Then staple them to the penguin as shown. Encourage each child to take her booklet home and share it with her family.

A penguin is a __bird__.

1

All About Penguins by __Karson__

A penguin can dive and __swim__.

2

A penguin is white and __black__.

3

A penguin eats __fish__.

4

Nonstandard measurement · · · · · · · · · · · · · · · Math

One Big Baby!

Share with youngsters that baby beluga whales, or calves, are approximately five feet long. Then place a five-foot length of masking tape on the floor. Provide access to a variety of nonstandard items youngsters can use for measuring, such as Unifix cubes, craft sticks, or straws. Have a small group of students work together to measure the length of tape with one of the provided supplies. Instruct the group to count the number of items used. Then have them repeat the process, measuring the calves' length with different items.

Seals and Bears

With this quick group game, your classroom is sure to sound like a gathering place for polar animals! Say a word from one of the lists shown. If the word rhymes with *bear,* prompt students to growl like a polar bear. If the word rhymes with seal, have students flap their "flippers" like a seal. Continue in the same way with other words from the lists below.

Rhymes with *bear:* chair, hair, wear, pear, their, care, dare, fair

Rhymes with *seal:* meal, deal, peel, real, feel, kneel, heel, wheel

real

Perfect Penguins

Provide access to black, white, yellow, and orange construction paper; scissors; and glue. Post pictures of penguins around your classroom. Then have each child make his own unique penguin using the supplies. Display the completed projects in a row at children's eye level to make a penguin parade. Invite youngsters to gather around the display. Then have a child point to the penguin that is first in the parade. Continue in the same way, having youngsters demonstrate their knowledge of other ordinal numbers.

Find reproducible activities on pages 48–49.

Puffin Pattern and Fish Cards
Use with "Let's Eat!" on page 40.

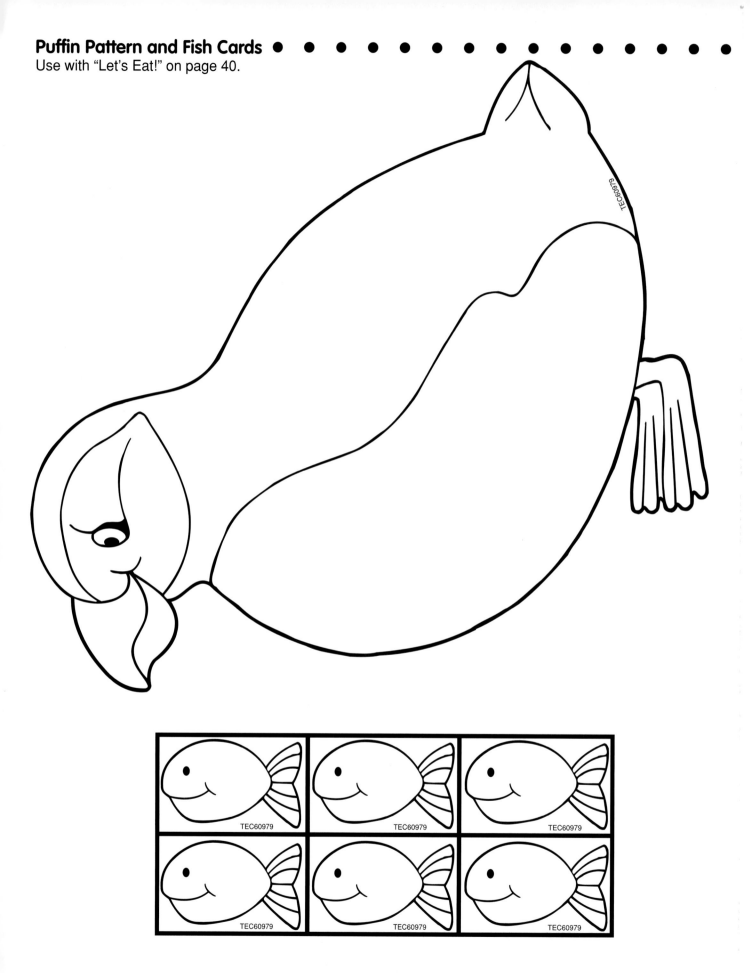

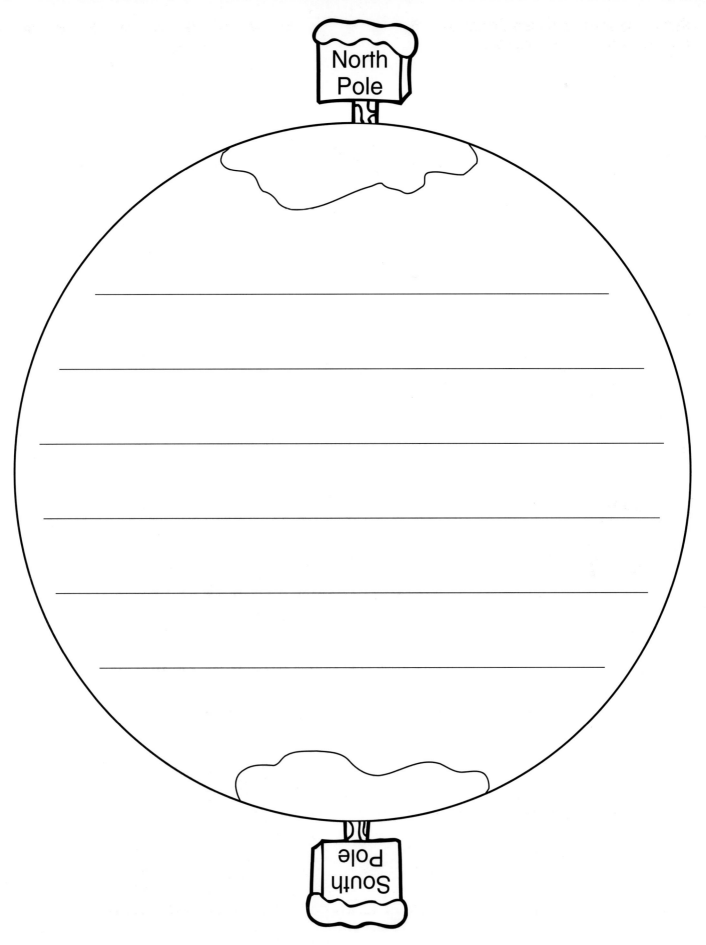

North Pole

South Pole

Note to the teacher: Use with "Polar Pals" on page 41.

Seal Patterns

Use with "Searching for Seals" on page 41.

TEC60979

TEC60979

Booklet Backing

Use with "Penguin Particulars" on page 42.

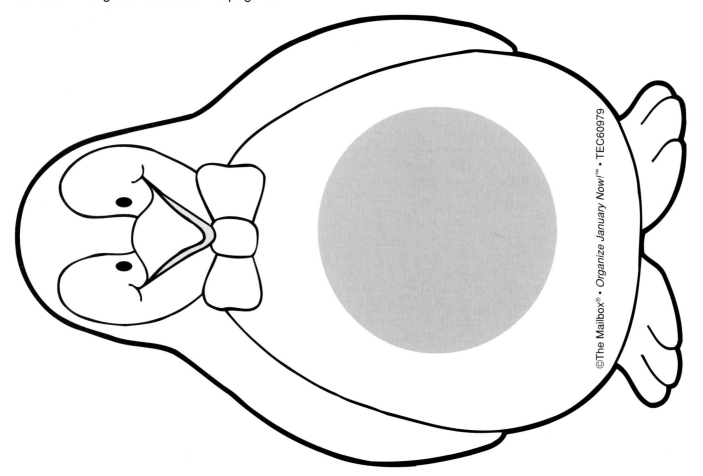

©The Mailbox® • *Organize January Now!*™ • TEC60979

Use with "Penguin Particulars" on page 42.

All About Penguins

by

____

A penguin is

a ________________.

1

A penguin

can dive and

________________.

2

A penguin

is white and

________________.

3

A penguin eats

________________.

4

Word Bank

fish black bird swim

Cool Pals

Name _____

✂ Cut.

🧴 Glue to match the pictures and the beginning letters.

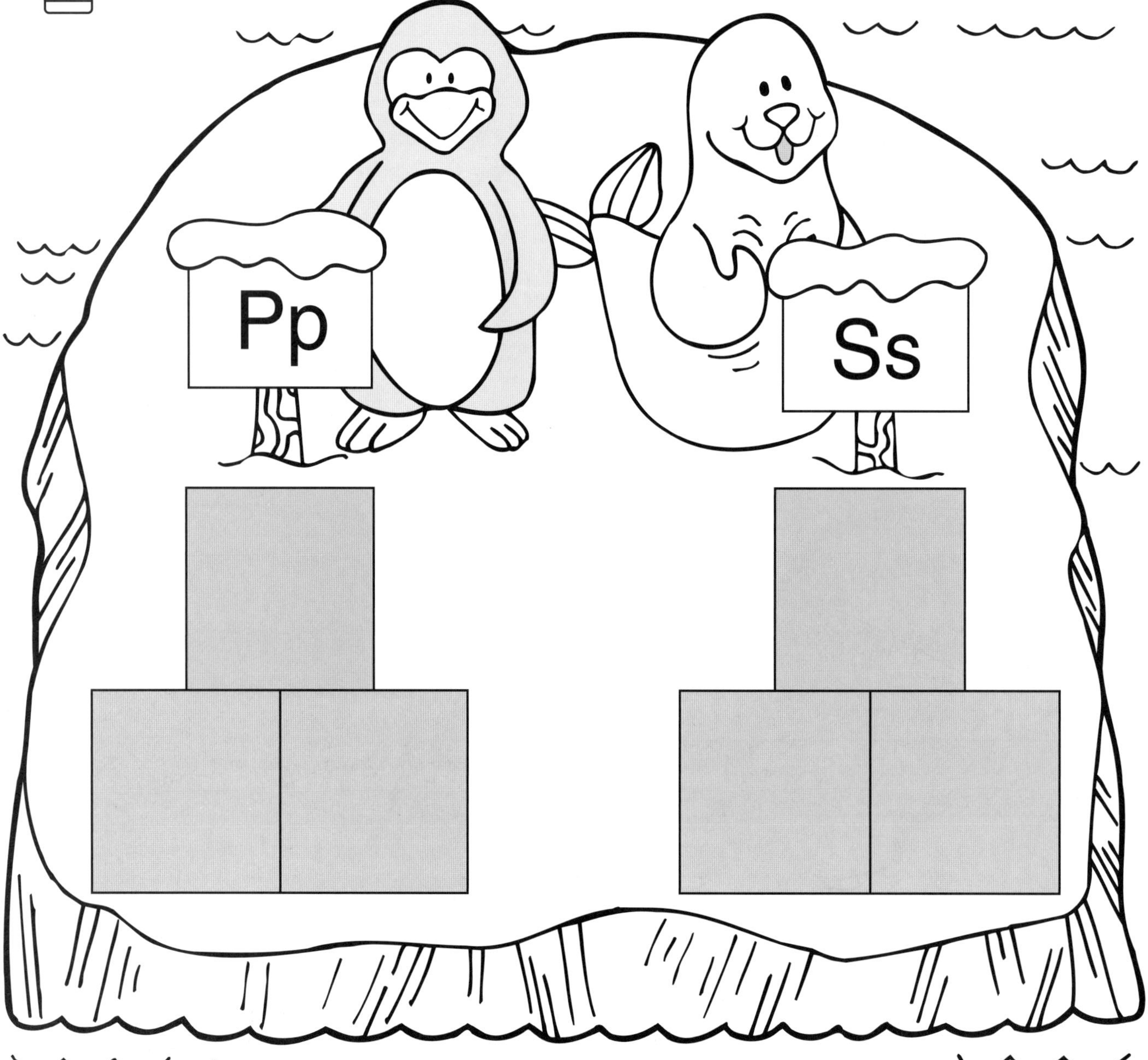

Pp

Ss

48 Initial Consonants: *p, s*

Fishing for Fives

Name _____

Count by fives.

Write how many.

_____   _____   _____   _____

_____   _____   _____

25

_____   _____   _____   _____

Arts & Crafts

Textured Polar Bear

These cute polar bears stay warm and toasty when you give them a coat—of oatmeal! To make a bear, cut out a copy of the polar bear pattern on page 52. Use a paintbrush to spread glue on the bear. Next, sprinkle dry oatmeal onto the wet glue. After the glue dries, glue a pom-pom nose and a construction paper eye to the bear.

A Chubby Snowman

To make a snowman, stuff a white paper lunch bag with shredded or crumbled newspaper. Once the bag is nearly full, fold down the opening and staple the top of the bag closed. Tie a strip of fabric around the middle of the bag to resemble a scarf. Then glue on construction paper facial features and a hat to complete this snowy friend!

Penguin on Ice

To make this cool pal, trace your hand (thumb and pinky outstretched) on black construction paper and cut along the resulting outline. Glue a white oval cutout to the hand cutout as shown. Attach hole reinforcers for eyes and an orange paper triangle for a beak. Next, glue the penguin to a sheet of blue construction paper. Then sponge-paint the lower portion of the paper with white tempera paint to resemble ice.

Sparkling Snow Globe

Create the globe by first coloring and cutting out a desired character from page 53 and gluing it to a six-inch blue construction paper circle. Glue small pieces of torn white paper around the character for snow. Next, peel the backing from a six-inch circle of clear covering and lay it atop the artwork (or laminate if desired). To make the snow globe's base, cut a half circle from construction paper and glue the globe to it as shown.

Polar Bear Pattern

Use with "Textured Polar Bear" on page 50.

TEC60979

TEC60979

TEC60979

TEC60979

TEC60979

Bulletin Boards &

Mount the title shown on a large paper cloud. Have each child write (or dictate) and illustrate a goal for the new year on a light-colored construction paper balloon. Mount the balloons below the title. Then connect the balloons with yarn or ribbon.

Mount an enlarged bear pattern (page 56), a "fiction" and a "nonfiction" sign, and the title on a board as shown. Each time you read a book aloud, ask a student volunteer to copy the title of the book on a large construction paper snowball and add an illustration. Later, have the class categorize the book as fiction or nonfiction and display the snowball accordingly.

Displays

Have each child decorate two construction paper mitten cutouts (patterns on page 57). Then have him personalize a red construction paper heart cutout. Connect each mitten pair with yarn. Then mount the mittens, hearts, and title as shown.

After discussing Martin Luther King Jr. and his dream, have each student think of a dream that she has for herself. Have each child write (or dictate) her thoughts on a sheet of white paper and then trim the paper to create a large thought bubble. Mount a student snapshot atop a larger piece of colorful construction paper. Display each student's photo along with her writing as shown.

TEC60979

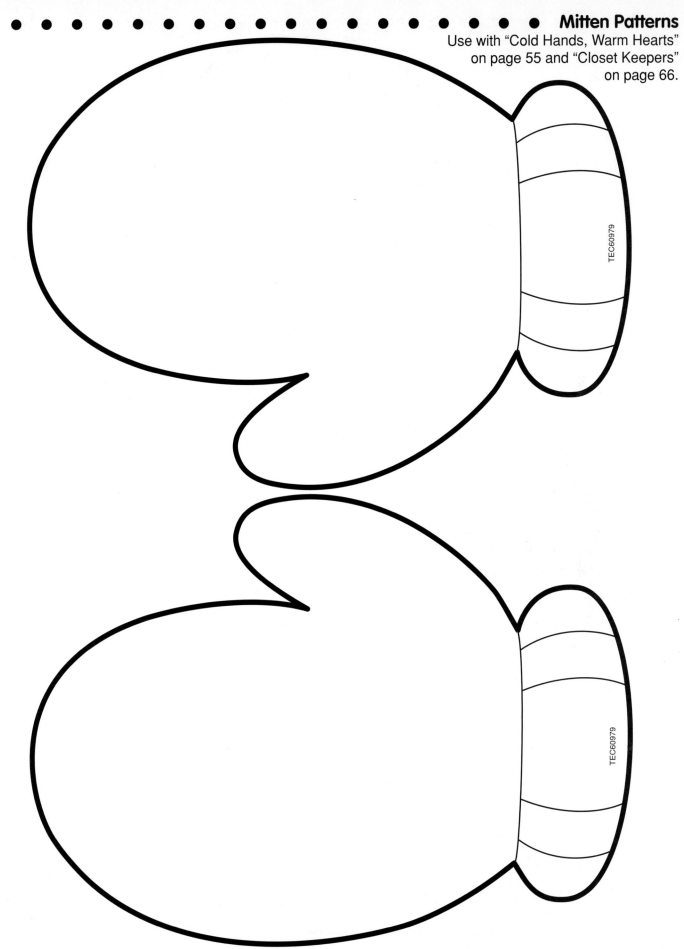

TEC60979

TEC60979

Centers

Math

Match numbers to sets

Snowpal Matching

To prepare, use the patterns on page 60 to make a supply of construction paper snowpal and hat cutouts. Program each snowpal with a different number of dots (buttons) and each hat with a matching numeral. Store the cutouts in a resealable plastic bag and place the bag at a center. A child chooses a snowpal, counts the buttons, and places the matching hat above the snowpal's head. He continues in this manner for the remaining cutouts. For more advanced students, have them sequence the numbers on the completed snowpals from least to greatest.

Syllables

Literacy

Cups of Cocoa

Color and cut out a copy of the picture cards on page 60 and mount each card on a slightly larger piece of white tagboard cut to resemble a marshmallow. Store the marshmallows in a resealable plastic bag. Label each of three nonbreakable mugs with a different number from 1 to 3. Place the mugs and the bag at a center. For each marshmallow, a student names the picture while clapping its word parts (syllables) and then places it in the corresponding mug.

In the Igloo

Choose a short- and long-vowel pair that you would like youngsters to practice. Cut out a copy of the igloo mat on page 61 and mount it atop a sheet of blue construction paper. Randomly program nine blocks with the short vowel and nine blocks with the long vowel. Then, on separate cards, write nine different words for the short vowel and nine different words for the long vowel. Place the cards, the mat, and 18 game markers at a center. To play, a child chooses a card, reads the word, and identifies the vowel as long or short. Then he covers a corresponding space on the mat with a marker. Play continues until each space is covered.

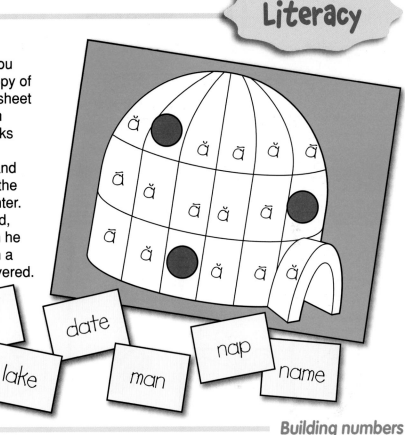

Literacy

Math

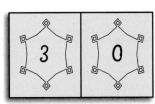
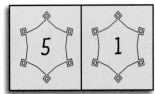
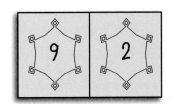

Greatest Numbers

After you have reviewed place-value concepts, this small-group center is a natural follow-up! Label each of ten construction paper snowflake cards (pattern on page 60) with a different number from 0 to 9. Store the cards in a winter hat and place the hat at a center along with individual whiteboards, wipe-off markers, and moist towelettes. Invite up to five students to the center. Each child removes two cards from the hat, arranges them to make the greatest two-digit number possible, and then writes her number on a whiteboard. Next, youngsters work together to compare all the two-digit numbers and determine which one is greatest. After returning their cards to the hat and wiping their boards clean, youngsters repeat the activity as time allows.

Snowpal and Hat Patterns
Use with "Snowpal Matching" on page 58.

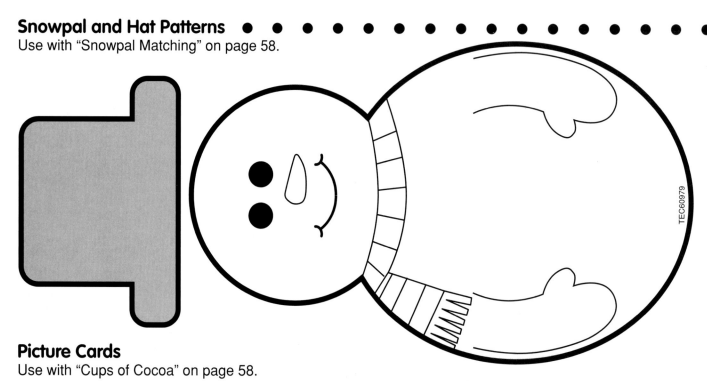

TEC60979

Picture Cards
Use with "Cups of Cocoa" on page 58.

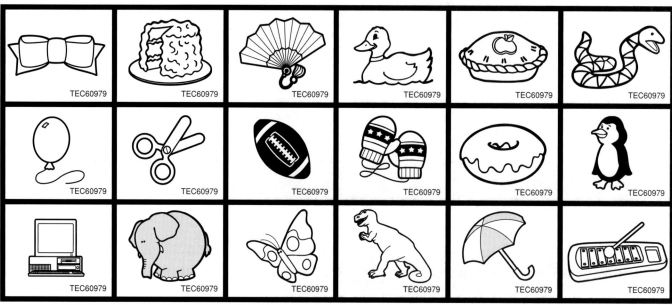

Snowflake Cards
Use with "Greatest Numbers" on page 59.

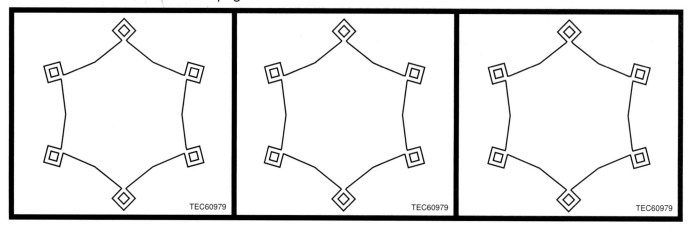

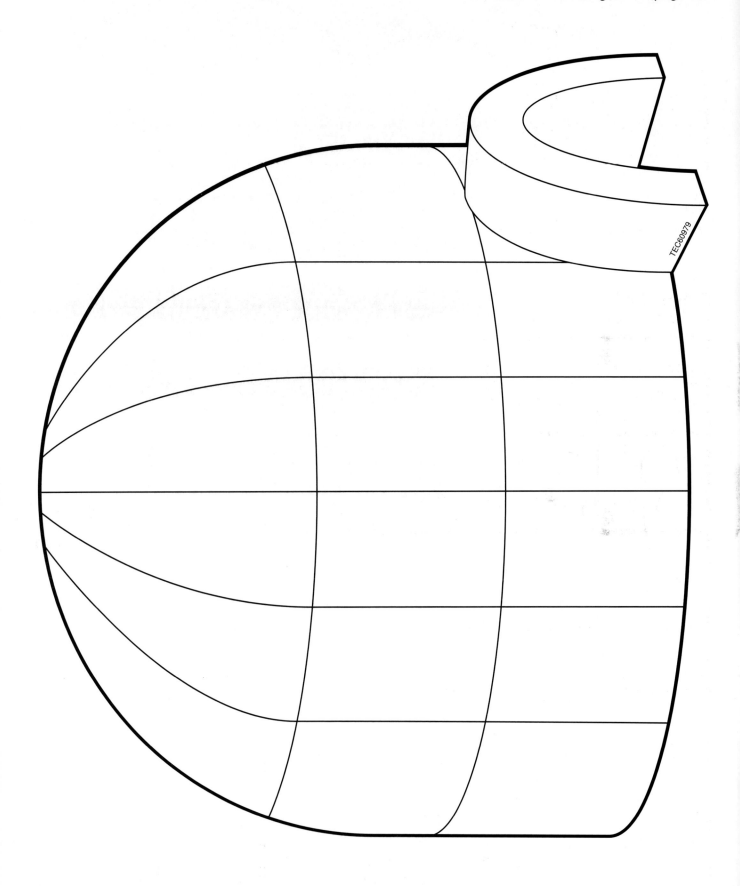

TEC60979

Games

Literacy

Letter identification

Iceberg Hop

Cut out several paper icebergs and label each one with a letter. Use clear covering to adhere the icebergs to the floor close enough together so that students will be able to hop from one to another. (For an outdoor version, draw and label icebergs on the pavement with sidewalk chalk.) Play some lively music while three or four children pretend to be polar animals and hop from iceberg to iceberg. Periodically stop the music and have each child identify the letter on her iceberg. Then restart the music for additional rounds of play.

Addition and subtraction facts

Math

Snowball Roll

Practice a flurry of skills with this wintry game. Sit with students in a circle. Roll a foam ball (snowball) to a student and announce a math problem. After the child answers, have her roll the snowball to another student. Then pose a different math problem to this student (or the same one if the previous child answered incorrectly). Continue in this manner until each child has had a turn.

Three plus four equals...

Gross motor

A Frosty Catch

For this cool indoor game, select a volunteer to be the scorekeeper and direct remaining students to each put on a pair of mittens and stand in a large circle. Have youngsters toss a foam ball (snowball) to each other while the scorekeeper silently counts the catches. When the ball is dropped, the scorekeeper announces the total number of catches. Then she and the last student who successfully caught the snowball switch roles. Continue play for a desired number of rounds.

Literacy

Vocabulary

Winter Lotto

This lotto game creates a blizzard of interest in winter-related words. Give each child a copy of the lotto board on page 64 and, depending on the ability of your group, a copy of the picture cards or word cards on page 65. Also gather a supply of mini marshmallows for students to use as markers. Have each child cut out the gameboard and cards. Then direct him to glue eight cards of his choice to his board. Cut apart an extra set of cards and place them in a bag. To play, draw a card and call out the picture name or word on it. Have each student use a mini marshmallow to cover the picture or word on his board. The first child to cover three spaces in a row calls out "Brrr!" After verifying the winner's lotto board, have students clear their boards for another round.

Winter Lotto

Free!

Name _____

Lotto Word Cards
Use with "Winter Lotto" on page 63.

sled	boots	snowflake	hat
mittens	penguin	ice skates	scarf
coat	ice	mug	snowman

The Marshmallow Mug

You can count on students warming right up to this cold-weather behavior incentive. Enlarge the mug pattern on page 67 on colored paper and display it in an easily accessible location. Each time the class shows outstanding behavior, have a student add a cotton ball or pom-pom marshmallow to the mug. When a predetermined number of marshmallows has been earned, reward youngsters with a hot cocoa party!

Frosty Attention Getter

You'll have all eyes on you with this management tip. When you need your students' attention, simply call out, "Iceberg!" At that point, have youngsters freeze and look at you. Then use this opportunity to give instructions.

"Iceberg!"

Closet Keepers

Boots, coats, and mittens are as tidy as can be when youngsters take charge of your classroom closet! Hang a length of string to represent a clothesline near the display of classroom helpers. Label two wooden clothespins "Closet Keeper" and clip them to the clothesline. Have each child cut out, decorate, and personalize a construction paper mitten (pattern on page 57). Store the mittens in a basket near the display. Each day, attach two mittens to the line and encourage those children to keep the closet tidy for the day.

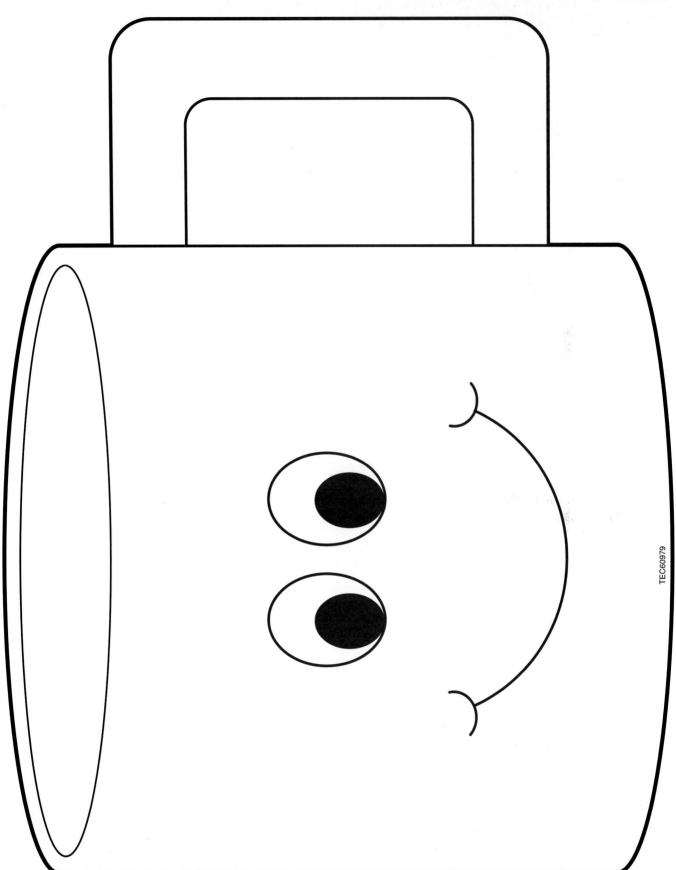

TEC60979

Time Fillers

Ten!
Happy
New Year!

Happy New Year!

Ring in the new year again and again with this quick and easy counting game! Have students stand in a circle. Designate one child to call out, "One!" Continue having children count off until the tenth youngster says his number and then yells, "Happy New Year!" Then have the tenth child take a seat on the floor. Have students continue counting to ten until everyone has had a chance to wish the class a happy New Year!

Snowflakes and Raindrops

When you have a few minutes to spare, pose this question to students: Do snowflakes and raindrops fall the same way? After a few youngsters share their thoughts, show students two identical pieces of paper. Crumple one piece to represent a raindrop and keep one piece flat to represent a snowflake. Encourage youngsters to watch as you stand and release both papers at the same time. Ask a student volunteer to describe the result. Then explain that a snowflake catches more air as it falls, so it floats down more slowly than a raindrop.

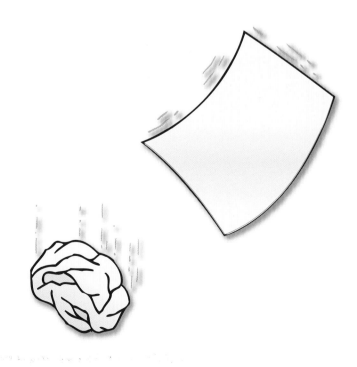

Don't Melt the Snowman!

Got a few extra minutes? Use this game to provide practice with spelling words. On the board, draw a line for each letter in a word you would like students to spell. Also draw a detailed snowman. Then challenge students to guess the letters in the word. Write each correct letter on the appropriate line. For each incorrect letter, erase one snowman part from the drawing. Challenge students to spell the word before the snowman is erased (melts)!

Dreamin'

Martin Luther King Jr. expressed his dreams for the future, and students will too with this activity. Remind students that Dr. King dreamed of the day when all people could live in peace. Then ask students to close their eyes and think about their dreams for the future. After reflection, invite students, in turn, to stand and share one dream as time allows.

Journal Prompts

- On New Year's Day, many people think about the past year. Write about your favorite memory of the year.

- Write about the things you want to learn in the upcoming year.

- What are the best things about winter? Why?

- Martin Luther King Jr. dreamed that all people would be treated fairly. How do you treat others fairly?

- Would you rather live where it snows every day or where it is sunny every day? Why?

- A magic snowflake lands on your shoulder and whispers in your ear. What does it say?

- Pretend you are a snowflake. Write about why you like being different from all the other snowflakes.

Use one or more of the following ideas and the snowflake pattern on page 72 to create a blizzard of writing interest!

- Have each child pretend she is a snowflake and write on a copy of the snowflake pattern about the neatest place she has landed. After she colors and cuts out the pattern, have her use glitter glue to add decorations. When the snowflakes are dry, hole-punch the top of each one and thread a yarn hanger through the hole. Then hang the snowflakes from the ceiling to decorate the room with your students' writing.

- Use the snowflake pattern for journal writing. Copy one of the last two journal prompts from the list above onto a copy of the snowflake pattern and add writing lines if desired; then make a class supply.

- Program a copy of the snowflake pattern with the numbers 1 through 3; then make a copy for each child. Have youngsters write three facts about winter.

When I was a snowflake, I landed on a dog's nose. I think I tickled him.

Prompts

January Time Capsule

Will youngsters remember winter when summer comes around? They will with this time capsule activity! Lead students in a discussion about weather, holidays, and events during winter. Then have each child write about the things that made this winter memorable. Stack the completed papers, roll them up, and slide them into a cardboard tube that you've labeled "Do not peek until the last week of school!" Mark your calendar to remind students to open the capsule, read their writings, and compare the past and present season.

Rebus Writing

Writing about building a snowman is lots of fun when youngsters use picture cards! Remind students that a story that uses pictures in place of some words is called a rebus. Then have each child color and cut out a copy of the picture cards on page 73. Help each child organize her cards to help her write the steps for creating a snowman. When she wants to use a word that matches a picture card, have her glue the card to her paper in place of the word. After she's finished writing, invite her to share her directions with a classmate.

Jill

How to Build a

1. Roll three balls of [snow].
2. Stack the balls.
3. Add [arms] and a [hat].
4. Push in a [carrot] for a nose and [buttons] for eyes and a mouth.

Snowflake Pattern

Use with the ideas at the bottom of page 70.

TEC60979

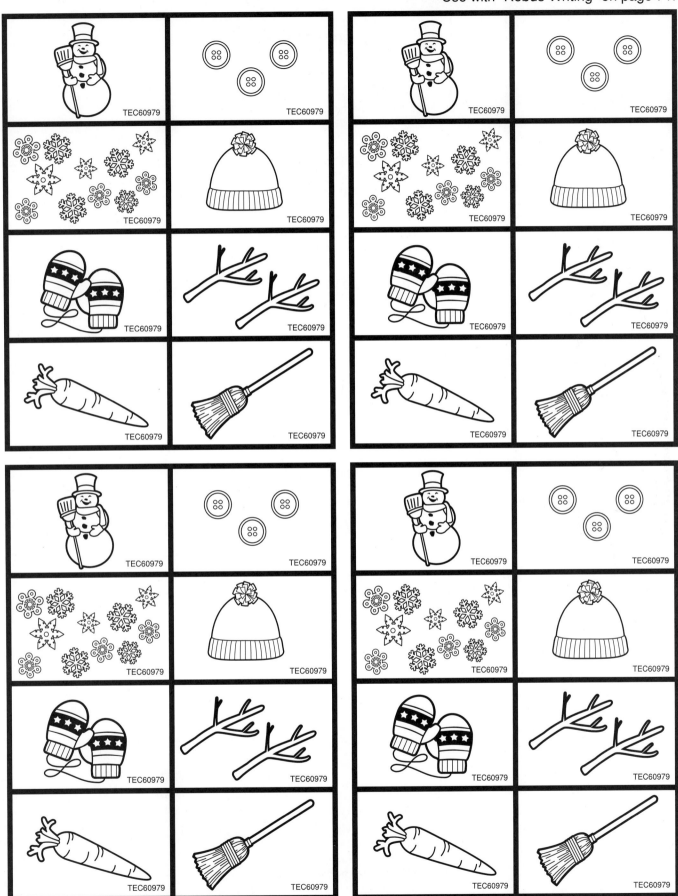

Let It Snow!

A ready-to-use center mat and cards for two different learning levels

Materials:
center mat to the right
center cards on page 77 (subtraction to 10 with manipulatives)
center cards on page 79 (subtraction to 18)
2 resealable plastic bags

Preparing the center:
Cut out the cards and place each set in a separate bag.

Using the center:
1. A child removes the cards from a bag and lays them faceup in the center area.
2. He puts a subtraction card on the rectangle.
3. He places the answer card beside it. (If he is using the first set of cards, he uses the snowflakes to help him subtract.)
4. To check his work, he turns over the subtraction card. If the numbers match, he removes the cards. If not, he turns the cards over and reworks the problem.
5. He repeats Steps 2–4 for each remaining card.

Let It Snow!

Put ☐.
Subtract.
Put ☐.
Check.

$10 - 4 =$ 6

$9 - 3 =$ $8 - 4 =$ $10 - 2 =$

Follow-Up
After a child completes the center activity for subtraction to 18, use the skill sheet on page 81 for more practice.

Let It Snow!

Put ☐.
Subtract.
Put ☐.
Check.

10 − 3 =	10 − 6 =	10 − 4 =
10 − 2 =	9 − 2 =	9 − 3 =
8 − 3 =	8 − 4 =	7 − 2 =

| 4 | 5 | 6 | 7 | 8 |

6

Let It Snow!
TEC60979

4

Let It Snow!
TEC60979

7

Let It Snow!
TEC60979

6

Let It Snow!
TEC60979

7

Let It Snow!
TEC60979

8

Let It Snow!
TEC60979

5

Let It Snow!
TEC60979

4

Let It Snow!
TEC60979

5

Let It Snow!
TEC60979

Let It Snow!
TEC60979

Let It Snow!
TEC60979

Let It Snow!
TEC60979

Let It Snow!
TEC60979

Let It Snow!
TEC60979

Let It Snow!
TEC60979

Let It Snow!
TEC60979

Let It Snow!
TEC60979

Let It Snow!
TEC60979

Let It Snow!
TEC60979

Let It Snow!
TEC60979

Let It Snow!
TEC60979

Let It Snow!
TEC60979

Let It Snow!
TEC60979

Let It Snow!
TEC60979

$18 - 9 =$	$9 - 9 =$	$15 - 9 =$
$15 - 7 =$	$13 - 7 =$	$12 - 8 =$
$11 - 4 =$	$12 - 9 =$	$9 - 8 =$
$14 - 6 =$	$13 - 8 =$	$11 - 9 =$

9	8	7	6	5
4	3	2	1	0

6

Let It Snow!
TEC60979

0

Let It Snow!
TEC60979

9

Let It Snow!
TEC60979

4

Let It Snow!
TEC60979

6

Let It Snow!
TEC60979

8

Let It Snow!
TEC60979

1

Let It Snow!
TEC60979

3

Let It Snow!
TEC60979

7

Let It Snow!
TEC60979

2

Let It Snow!
TEC60979

5

Let It Snow!
TEC60979

8

Let It Snow!
TEC60979

Let It Snow!
TEC60979

Let It Snow!
TEC60979

Let It Snow!
TEC60979

Let It Snow!
TEC60979

Let It Snow!
TEC60979

Let It Snow!
TEC60979

Let It Snow!
TEC60979

Let It Snow!
TEC60979

Let It Snow!
TEC60979

Let It Snow!
TEC60979

Window Shopping

Name _____

Subtract. 🖍️ Color by the code.

18 − 9	16 − 9	17 − 8	15 − 9
15 − 7	14 − 8	17 − 9	
13 − 6	16 − 8	12 − 5	

Color Code

6 — blue   7 — red

8 — green   9 — orange

The Polar Plunge

A ready-to-use center mat and cards for two different learning levels

Sequencing a story in four steps

Materials:
center mat to the right
picture cards on page 85
sentence cards on page 87
6 resealable plastic bags

Preparing the center:
Cut out the cards and place each color-coded set in a separate bag.

Using the center:

1. A student removes the cards from a bag and lays them faceup in the center area.
2. She places the cards on the mat in the correct sequence.
3. To check her work, she flips the cards over. If the numbers on the backs of the cards are in order, her work is complete. If not, she reorders the cards so they are arranged correctly.
4. She places the completed story back in the bag.
5. She repeats Steps 2–5 for each bag.

Follow-Up
After a student completes the center activity for sequencing pictures, use the skill sheet on page 89 for more practice.

The Polar Plunge

Put the cards in order.

Check.

84

1

The Polar Plunge
TEC60979

1

The Polar Plunge
TEC60979

1

The Polar Plunge
TEC60979

2

The Polar Plunge
TEC60979

2

The Polar Plunge
TEC60979

2

The Polar Plunge
TEC60979

3

The Polar Plunge
TEC60979

3

The Polar Plunge
TEC60979

3

The Polar Plunge
TEC60979

4

The Polar Plunge
TEC60979

4

The Polar Plunge
TEC60979

4

The Polar Plunge
TEC60979

Bear runs to the water.	Bear puts on a coat.	Bear puts a hat in the box.
Then Bear dives in.	Then Bear puts on a hat.	He wraps the box.
He makes a big splash!	Finally, Bear puts on his boots.	He puts a bow on top.
Bear is under the water.	Bear goes sledding.	He gives the gift to a friend.

1

The Polar Plunge
TEC60979

1

The Polar Plunge
TEC60979

1

The Polar Plunge
TEC60979

2

The Polar Plunge
TEC60979

2

The Polar Plunge
TEC60979

2

The Polar Plunge
TEC60979

3

The Polar Plunge
TEC60979

3

The Polar Plunge
TEC60979

3

The Polar Plunge
TEC60979

4

The Polar Plunge
TEC60979

4

The Polar Plunge
TEC60979

4

The Polar Plunge
TEC60979

A Chilly Treat!

Name _____

✂ Cut. Put the pictures in order.

🧴 Glue.

1	2	3	4

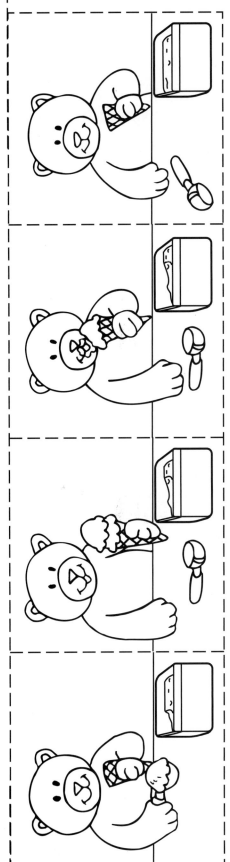

©The Mailbox® • *Organize January Now!*™ • TEC60979

Sequencing a Story **89**

Patchwork Mitten

Name _____

✂ Cut.

🧴 Glue the pictures that start with **m**.

©The Mailbox® • *Organize January Now!*™ • TEC60979

Having a Ball!

Name _____

✏️ Write the matching lowercase letter.

Use the letters on the small snowball to help you.

B _____   G _____

F _____   L _____

A _____   T _____

D _____   R _____

E _____   H _____

I _____   M _____

l r i
a
h e d
f m
b g
t

Uppercase and Lowercase Letters 91

Happy New Year

Name

Cut.

Glue to match the vowel sounds.

Short Vowels: a, o

Winter's Here!

Name _____

✎ Write a **.** or a **?** in each box.

If the sentence ends with a **?**, circle the asking word.

How does Bear get ready for winter ☐

He eats a lot of food ☐

He looks for a warm place to sleep ☐

Where will Bear sleep ☐

Bear will sleep in a cave ☐

Does he sleep all winter ☐

Will he be hungry ☐

In the spring, Bear will wake up to eat ☐

Winter Wear for Sale!

Name _____

✂ Cut.

Glue to match the money amount.

5¢	1¢
1¢	5¢
5¢	1¢

Identifying Pennies and Nickels

94

Frosty Skating

Name _____

Write each set of numbers from least to greatest.

39   11   100

____ ____ ____

90   14   66

____ ____ ____

68   41   24

____ ____ ____

23   84   40

____ ____ ____

71   17   97

____ ____ ____

60   58   53

____ ____ ____

● ● ● ● Warming Up!

Name _____

Add or subtract.

 Color by the code.

	8 +	9 −	8 − 2	8 + 4
	3	1		

9 −	11 − 2	12 − 7	7 + 3

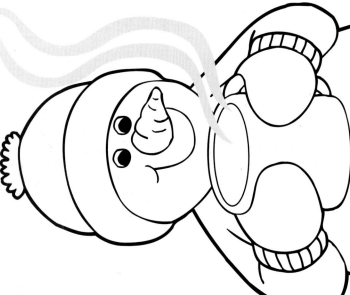

Color Code
5 or 6 — red
7 or 8 — blue
9 or 10 — yellow
11 or 12 — green

12 − 4	2 + 9	6 + 6

4 + 6	4 + 3	10 − 5

Addition and Subtraction Facts to 12